TACOS

60 recipes for fillings, salsas & sides

**Felipe Fuentes Cruz
& Ben Fordham**

Photography by
Peter Cassidy

RYLAND PETERS & SMALL
LONDON • NEW YORK

Senior Designer Toni Kay
Senior Editor Abi Waters
Head of Production Patricia Harrington
Creative Director Leslie Harrington
Editorial Director Julia Charles

Food Stylist Emily Kydd
Prop Stylist Luis Peral
Indexer Cathy Heath

First published in 2024
by Ryland Peters & Small
20–21 Jockey's Fields
London WC1R 4BW
and
341 E 116th St
New York NY 10029

www.rylandpeters.com

10 9 8 7 6 5 4 3 2 1

The recipes in this book have previously appeared in *Everyone Loves Tacos* and *Real Mexican Food* by Felipe Fuentes Cruz and Ben Fordham

ISBN: 978-1-78879-589-0

Printed in China

A CIP record for this book is available from the British Library.
US Library of Congress Cataloging-in-Publication Data has been applied for.

NOTES

• We hope that you'll be making lots of your own tortillas, however, we know that you'll sometimes need to use the store-bought variety. The standard size is about 15 cm/6 inches, so we have assumed that size for the recipes. However, if you are making them yourself you'll need to adjust the size you make accordingly.

• Whether to use flour or corn tortillas (or even mezcla, which is a combination of both) is really up to you. We generally favour corn (particularly for fish and seafood fillings), but we would certainly opt for flour at breakfast time.

• Both British (Metric) and American (Imperial plus US cups) ingredients measurements are included in these recipes for your convenience, however it is important to work with one set of measurements and not alternate between the two within a recipe.

• All spoon measurements are level unless otherwise specified.

• All eggs are medium (UK) or large (US), unless specified as large, in which case US extra-large should be used. Uncooked or partially cooked eggs should not be served to the very old, frail, young children, pregnant women or those with compromised immune systems.

• When a recipe calls for the grated zest of citrus fruit, buy unwaxed fruit and wash well before using. If you can only find treated fruit, scrub well in warm soapy water before using.

• We usually leave the seeds in our chillies/chiles but, if you prefer a milder taste, remove the seeds to tone down the heat.

CONTENTS

INTRODUCTION

The taco is one of the pillars of Mexican cuisine and has rightly become one of the most famous dishes associated with it. It's versatility makes it a much-loved staple and has seen a huge growth in popularity due to Taco Tuesdays and the fact it can be easily personalized to every taste and occasion. In it's most basic form, a taco is made of a corn or flour tortilla, folded or rolled around a filling (meat, fish or veg) and a salsa – and that is about as simple and delicious as it gets.

In Mexico, the taco has become an integral part of the food prepared in every household. Whichever village, town or city you visit when travelling around the country, there will be a taco stall, taco truck or *taqueria* (taco restaurant) – and in every one of those you will find exciting regional variations. For example, *Tacos de camaron* (grilled or fried prawns/shrimp) and *Tacos de pescado* (fish tacos) originated in Baja California. Coahuila in the north of Mexico is where a traditional vegetarian *Tacos laguneros* came from, while *Tacos al pastor* are associated with the streets of Mexico City, *Tacos de chilorio* (pork) with Sinaloa, marinated pork tacos from the Yucatan, and *Tacos de canasta* in Tlaxcala. In all these regional varieties, what links them is their simplicity.

When you are making tacos at home, you will first need to decide on your principal filling, then it is all about the garnishes and salsas. Here you can mix and match the flavours to your heart's content. There are some well-established classics like pork and pineapple or lamb with avocado, but as you will see with the recipes in this book, the combinations are endless. Choose from a traditional Chipotle Chicken Tacos (see page 33) or Beef Brisket Barbacoa Tacos (see page 37) or mix things up a bit and try the Lobster and Crab Fritter Tacos (see page 61) or the Deep-fried Fresh Tuna Tacos (see page 54). And don't stop there – create your own wonderfully tasty tacos by switching up the salsas and sides and trying something new. Choose from a Tropical Pineapple Salsa (see page 112) or some zingy Lime and Red Onion Salsa (see page 109) to name just a few.

Mexican food comes in all shapes and sizes, and tacos brings the fun and flavour to the extreme through these tasty taco recipes.

HOW TO MAKE CORN TORTILLAS

Here is your basic tool – the humble corn tortilla. There is nothing complicated about this recipe but if this is your first time making tortillas, you will probably get it wrong a few times before you get it right. Stick with it though, as it is just a knack that comes with practice and experience and the results will transform any taco!

Masa harina is a flour made from grinding dried field corn or maize. It is available from online suppliers if you cannot find it in your supermarket.

200 g/2 cups masa harina
(fine yellow cornflour/maize)
300 ml/1¼ cups warm water
¼ tsp sea salt
clean plastic bag
tortilla press (optional), or a large saucepan

MAKES 10 TORTILLAS, 8 CM/3¼ INCHES IN DIAMETER

Put the masa harina, water and salt in a mixing bowl and mix well for 3–5 minutes until you have a smooth, pliable dough. Divide the mixture into ten equal pieces and roll into balls.

Open up a plastic bag by cutting down each side so that you have one, flat piece. Place one ball of dough in the middle of the plastic bag and place this in the middle of the open tortilla press, if using one. Fold the bag in half over the dough, close the tortilla press and push the handle down firmly to compress the dough as much as possible.

Open the tortilla press and check that the tortilla is nice and thin. Compress again if necessary. Very carefully peel back the

plastic from the top of the dough, making sure the dough does not tear, then flip it over in your hand so that it is dough-side-down in your hand and gently peel back the remaining plastic.

If you don't have a tortilla press, place a large saucepan on top of the plastic-covered dough, repeatedly pressing down firmly and evenly. Now set the pan aside and pat firmly a few times with the palm of your hand to flatten the dough even further. Gently peel off the plastic as above.

Repeat this process until you have made ten tortillas.

To cook, heat a non-stick frying pan/skillet over a medium heat (don't add any oil), then cook each tortilla for 1 minute on each side until cooked through. To keep the tortillas warm, place them on a clean kitchen towel and fold the cloth over to cover them.

A good tortilla is not too thick and not too thin. If it is too thin, it will break when trying to peel the plastic off and if it is too thick, it won't cook evenly. The best tortilla should fluff up when cooked.

CHAPTER 1

BREAKFAST & BRUNCH

PINTO BEAN & CHORIZO TACOS

Pinto beans are a staple of Mexican cooking and a great source of high-quality fibre and protein. You will be hard pushed to find any restaurant in Mexico that will not serve its own version of this classic.

175 g/1 cup dried pinto beans,
    soaked overnight and drained
1 tbsp vegetable oil
150 g/5 oz. chorizo, chopped
    or sliced
¼ onion, finely chopped
1 small garlic clove, finely chopped
2 tsp paprika
½ tsp salt

Serve with
8-12 flour or corn tortillas, warmed
200 g/7 oz. queso fresco or
    feta cheese, crumbled (optional)
freshly chopped coriander/cilantro
    (optional)
150 g/5 oz. chorizo, sliced
Toasted Chile de Árbol Salsa
    (see page 115)

SERVES 4–6

Place the soaked and drained pinto beans in a deep saucepan with 1.5 litres/6 cups of fresh water. Bring to the boil and boil rapidly for 10 minutes, then turn the heat down to low and cook for 2-2½ hours. Put a lid on the saucepan but do not cover fully – just tilt the lid so that there is a gap to allow steam to escape. Keep an eye on it just in case you need to add a little more water. At the end, you should be able to crush the beans easily between your fingers – but please don't try this when they are hot! If they still have some bite, cook for a little longer, adding more water if necessary.

Heat the oil in a medium saucepan, add the chorizo pieces, onion and garlic and sweat for about 1 minute. Add the cooked beans and the paprika and cook for 10 minutes over a medium-low heat, using a potato masher to mash the beans continuously. The beans and chorizo should not be runny. Add the salt to taste.

Fill the warmed tortillas with the refried bean and chorizo mixture and stack next to each other on a serving plate. Sprinkle the cheese and coriander, if using, onto each taco and serve with the additional chorizo and salsa alongside.

EGGS & HAM TACOS

Most Mexican households start their day with a breakfast of eggs. As with many such recipes, it is the combination of creamy eggs with a zesty salsa that provides the perfect balance for the morning.

6 eggs

2 tbsp vegetable oil

125 g/4½ oz. (6–8 thin slices) ham, chopped into pieces

1 tsp salt

Salsa verde

1–2 fresh green chillies/chiles

2 garlic cloves, peeled

2–3 fresh tomatillos, husks removed

1 tsp rock salt

3 tbsp freshly chopped coriander/cilantro

½ onion, chopped

Serve with

8–12 flour or corn tortillas, warmed

100 g/1 cup grated/shredded cheese (ideally Monterey Jack or mild Cheddar)

SERVES 3–4

First, prepare the salsa verde. Preheat the oven to 200°C/400°F/Gas 6. Put the chillies, garlic and fresh tomatillos on a baking sheet and roast for 20 minutes or until charred. Halve the chillies and scoop out and discard the seeds. Using a molcajete or pestle and mortar, pound the chillies, garlic and salt into a paste. Add the tomatillos and grind until well mixed. Add the coriander and onion and stir with a spoon. Add a little water or extra salt, if required.

Break the eggs into a bowl, add 1 tablespoon of the salsa verde and whisk for about 30 seconds.

Heat the oil in a saucepan over a low-medium heat, then add the chopped ham and the salt and sauté for a few seconds. Add the beaten eggs and cook for about 1–2 minutes, stirring gently.

While the eggs are cooking, heat the tortillas. Place the warmed tortillas on the table together with the eggs, a bowl of extra salsa verde and the grated cheese, and let everyone help themselves.

MEXICAN-STYLE EGG TACOS

This is Mexican-style scrambled eggs, featuring the vibrant colours of the Mexican flag. This recipe's use of simple, fresh ingredients creates a classic fusion of flavours that is very characteristic of Mexican cuisine.

6 eggs
2 tbsp vegetable oil
¼ onion, finely chopped
1 large tomato, finely chopped
4 tsp freshly chopped coriander/
    cilantro
2 serrano chillies/chiles, deseeded
    and finely chopped
1 tsp salt

Serve with
6–8 flour or corn tortillas, warmed
your choice of salsa (see pages
    108–125)

SERVES 3–4

Break the eggs into a bowl and whisk for 30 seconds.

Heat the oil in a saucepan, then sauté the onion, tomato, coriander, chillies and salt for a few seconds.

Add the eggs and cook over a low-medium heat for about 1-2 minutes, stirring slowly, until creamy.

While the eggs are cooking, heat the tortillas. Serve on the table with the eggs and salsas and let everyone help themselves.

Note: Salsa verde (see page 14) also works well with eggs and is a lot gentler on your tastebuds than a fiery chilli salsa if preferred.

ALL-DAY NEW POTATO TACOS

Here they are in the breakfast category but, as the name suggests, these provide a great addition to any meal whatever the time of day. Ignore the tortillas and they become a great side to every Mexican dish.

500 g/1 lb. 2 oz. new potatoes
2 tbsp vegetable oil
½ red onion, finely chopped
3 tbsp freshly chopped parsley
1 red chilli/chile, deseeded and
    thinly sliced (optional)
a pinch of white pepper
1 tsp salt

Serve with
8–12 flour or corn tortillas, warmed
125 g/4½ oz. Cheddar cheese,
    cut into cubes
2 fresh avocados, peeled, stoned/
    pitted and diced or cut into strips
Roasted Cherry Tomatoes
    (see page 95)

SERVES 4

Place the potatoes in a saucepan with 1.5 litres/6 cups of boiling water and boil for 15 minutes. Remove from the heat, drain the potatoes and allow them to cool.

Cut the potatoes in half and then cut each half into thin slices.

Put a saucepan over a high heat, add the oil and, when hot, add the cooked sliced potatoes. Fry gently for 2–3 minutes until they start to colour.

Add the red onion, parsley, chilli (if using), white pepper and salt and sauté them for 1 minute.

Heap on top of the tortillas and garnish with small cubes of Cheddar cheese, the avocado and Roasted Cherry Tomatoes.

BLT TACOS

The taco part of this recipe is as simple as it gets, but the combination of crispy bacon with a fresh salsa is what makes this truly spectacular. To make this even fresher and healthier, we have swapped out the traditional tortillas and are using the 'L' part of the 'BLT' as the wrap. Think light lunch on a hot, summer's day, or refreshing appetizer before a bbq feast.

2 tsp vegetable oil
8 rashers/slices of bacon
1 romaine lettuce
2 tomatoes, chopped
1 tbsp freshly chopped parsley

Cucumber & chilli salsa

1 cucumber – ¾ peeled, sliced in half lengthwise, seeds removed and cut into half-moons and final ¼ left whole
freshly squeezed juice of 3 lemons
1 Thai chilli/chile
¼ tsp salt
¼ tsp freshly ground black pepper
½ red onion, thinly sliced
2 tbsp freshly chopped coriander/cilantro

SERVES 3–4

First, make the salsa. Blend the lemon juice with the chilli, the quarter of the cucumber, salt and pepper. Place the sliced cucumber and onion on a platter, cover with the lemon juice and chilli mixture and the chopped coriander and mix well. Cover and put it in the refrigerator until you are ready to serve.

Place the vegetable oil in a frying pan/skillet over a medium-high heat and fry the bacon for about 6–7 minutes. Turn the bacon over several times. Put the bacon on a plate lined with paper towels to absorb any excess oil.

Wash the lettuce leaves and remove the stems. Take a leaf of lettuce and place it in a bowl shape on a plate. Put a rasher/slice or two of bacon in the middle of the leaf, top with some tomato and spoon over the salsa. Scatter over the parsley to finish.

BURGER TACOS

Putting some vegetables in the meat mixture for these burgers bumps up the nutrition and the mint adds something a bit special.

500 g/1 lb. 2 oz. minced/ground beef
½ yellow (bell) pepper, finely chopped
½ red (bell) pepper, finely chopped
2 garlic cloves, finely chopped
¼ red onion, finely chopped
½ courgette/zucchini, finely chopped
10 fresh mint leaves, finely chopped
½ tsp salt
½ tsp freshly ground black pepper
¼ tsp ground cumin

Chipotle ketchup
600 ml/2½ cups tomato ketchup
1 tbsp freshly chopped ginger
1 tbsp chopped chipotle chilli/chile

Serve with
8 slices of Cheddar cheese
8 flour or corn tortillas, warmed
8 romaine lettuce leaves
1 tomato, thinly sliced
1 red onion, thinly sliced

SERVES 4

First make the chipotle ketchup. Place all the ingredients in a blender with 90 ml/6 tablespoons water and blend for 1–2 minutes. Refrigerate until you are ready to use.

Place the minced beef, peppers, garlic, onion, courgette, mint, salt, pepper and cumin in a mixing bowl and mix together well. Divide the mixture into four equal portions and form a burger with each one. Cook them in a griddle pan or frying pan/skillet for 3–4 minutes on each side, turning occasionally to ensure the meat is cooked through.

When cooked, remove from the heat and top each burger with a slice of Cheddar cheese.

Place a tortilla on a plate, layer on a lettuce leaf, then the burger with cheese, and top with tomato and red onion. Serve with the bowl of Chipotle Ketchup for people to serve themselves. Or if you wish, you can smear the ketchup over the tortillas before laying on the lettuce, burger and other toppings.

Note: To make these tacos easier to eat, you can cut them in half horizontally to make a thinner burger and stack as above.

SPINACH, CHORIZO & POTATO TACOS

The chorizo in these tasty tacos adds a touch of spice and great colour to the potatoes and spinach.

2 tbsp vegetable oil
100 g/3½ oz. chorizo, cut into
    5-mm/¼-inch slices
1 medium potato, peeled and
    cut into small strips
1 red onion, thinly sliced
100 g/2 cups baby spinach leaves
a pinch of salt
a pinch of white pepper

Serve with
a bunch of watercress
100 g/3½ oz. radishes, thinly sliced
5-6 flour or corn tortillas, warmed
200 g/1½ cups crumbled queso
    fresco or feta cheese
Smoked Chipotle Salsa
    (see page 121)

SERVES 2–3

Heat the oil in a saucepan over a medium heat, add the chorizo slices and cook for 2 minutes. Then add the potato strips and fry for 6–8 minutes until cooked. Add the onion, spinach, salt and white pepper and cook for another 1–2 minutes, then put them to one side.

Place the watercress and radish slices in two separate bowls on the table. Place the chorizo mixture in the middle of the warmed tortillas and add the crumbled cheese. Add a dollop of salsa and serve.

CHAPTER 2

MEAT

CHICKEN TINGA TACOS

Chicken Tinga is a one-pot (albeit used several times) versatile dish of shredded chicken that is quick and easy to make.

500 g/1 lb. 2 oz. skinless, boneless chicken breasts
1 large onion, chopped
3 tomatoes, cut into wedges
2 garlic cloves, peeled
2 tbsp chipotle paste
¾ tsp white pepper
1 tbsp paprika
1½ tsp salt
2 tbsp vegetable oil

Serve with
12 flour or corn tortillas, warmed
½ romaine lettuce, shredded
1 bunch of radishes, sliced
½ red onion, sliced
150 ml/⅔ cup sour cream
200 g/7 oz. feta cheese, crumbled

SERVES 3–4

Place the chicken in a small saucepan with 1 litre/4 cups water, bring to the boil, then simmer for 10 minutes. Skim the froth from the top if necessary. Remove the saucepan from the heat. Remove the chicken from the pan and put to one side to cool. Pour the broth into a separate bowl and reserve for later. When the chicken is cool enough to handle, shred into small pieces.

In the now-empty saucepan, place 20 g/¼ cup of the chopped onion, the tomatoes and garlic and 500 ml/2 cups water, bring to the boil, then simmer for 5 minutes. Drain, discard the water and leave to cool. Once cooled, place in a blender with the chipotle paste, white pepper, paprika and salt and blend for 1 minute until completely smooth.

Take the saucepan again and heat the oil, then add the remaining chopped onion. Sauté for 1 minute, then add the shredded chicken and the mixture from the blender and cook for another minute. Add 125 ml/½ cup of the reserved chicken broth and simmer over a low heat for 15 minutes.

Place a generous spoonful of chicken tinga on top of each warmed tortilla. Top up with the lettuce, radishes, red onion, sour cream and finally the crumbled feta cheese.

CHICKEN TAQUITOS

Taquitos (also known as a *flauta*) are tacos filled with various ingredients, rolled like a cigar, then fried until crisp.

2 boneless, skinless
  chicken breasts
2 garlic cloves, crushed
¼ onion, chopped
¼ tsp salt
12 corn tortillas
vegetable oil, for frying

Serve with
½ romaine lettuce,
  shredded
Pico de Gallo (see page 119)
25 ml/½ cup sour cream
200 g/7 oz. queso fresco
  or feta cheese
handful of freshly chopped
  coriander/cilantro
36 cocktail sticks/toothpicks

SERVES 3–4

Pour 1 litre/4 cups water into a saucepan and bring to the boil. Add the chicken, garlic, onion and salt and simmer for 7–8 minutes or until the chicken is completely cooked. Lift out the chicken and set aside to cool. Reserve the onion and garlic, and discard the cooking liquid. Shred the cooled chicken and mix with the cooked onion and garlic.

Heat one tortilla in a dry, non-stick frying pan/skillet until softened and flexible. Spoon a little shredded chicken onto the warmed tortilla, just slightly to the side of centre. Roll the tortilla into a cylinder and secure it with 3 cocktail sticks/toothpicks, gently pushing them through the cylinder. Repeat with all the remaining tortillas and chicken.

Pour vegetable oil into a deep frying pan to a depth of about 2 cm/¾ inches. Heat over a medium heat until the oil is hot but not smoking. Carefully drop in the taquitos in batches of 3–4 and fry for 12 minutes until golden, turning gently and occasionally to prevent them from burning.

Using tongs or a slotted spoon, remove the taquitos from the pan and allow to drain on paper towels. When the taquitos are cool enough to handle, remove the cocktail sticks/toothpicks. Put a little shredded lettuce on each plate, add 3–4 taquitos, top with Pico de Gallo, sour cream, cheese and coriander.

CHIPOTLE CHICKEN TACOS

Although tacos are at the heart of Mexican cooking, chicken is not as common a filling as pork or beef, but this chipotle flavoured filling is too good to miss.

400 g/14 oz. chicken breast fillets

Chipotle marinade
1 tbsp Chipotle chilli paste
1 tsp ground cinnamon
1 tsp ground cumin
3 garlic cloves
1 tbsp dried oregano
1 tbsp paprika
½ tsp sea salt
125 ml/½ cup vegetable oil

Serve with
8 flour or corn tortillas, warmed
a handful of shredded
   Romaine lettuce
Pico de Gallo (see page 119)
sour cream

SERVES 4

Put all the marinade ingredients and 125 ml/ ½ cup water in a food processor and blend until smooth. Put the chicken breast in a bowl, add the marinade and mix well. Cover, refrigerate and marinate for 2–4 hours.

When you are ready to start cooking, preheat the grill/broiler to high.

Grill/broil the chicken for about 10 minutes, turning halfway through, until cooked through, then cut it into strips.

Layer up the ingredients over the warmed tortillas: lettuce, Pico de Gallo, sour cream and finish with the chicken.

ROASTED PORK BELLY TACOS

In Mexico, these are known as *tacos de carnitas,* meaning 'little meats' and refers to the fact that you first slow-cook the meat, and then chop it into small pieces before crisping it up in a pan at the last minute. Add in the juice and zest of the orange and you have a really special, citrus-sweet flavour.

1 kg/2¼ lb. pork belly
2½ tsp salt
2 tbsp vegetable oil
zest and juice of 2 oranges

Serve with

12 flour or corn tortillas, warmed
Pico de Gallo (see page 119)
Chipotle Slaw (see page 87)
2–3 spring onions/scallions,
    thinly sliced
50 g/2 oz radishes, thinly sliced
Apple Salsa (see page 113)

SERVES 3–4

Preheat the oven to 220°C/425°F/Gas 7.

Pour 500 ml/2 cups water into a deep roasting tray. Place a rack in the roasting tray, then place the pork on the rack to prevent it touching the bottom of the tray. Cover the pork evenly with 2 teaspoons of the salt. Cover the whole container with a lid or foil, put it in the preheated oven and cook for 1½ hours.

When the pork is cooked through, transfer to a chopping board. Discard any bones or cartilage and chop the meat into strips about 5 mm/¼ inch thick and 5 cm/2 inches long.

Heat the oil in a saucepan, add the meat and sauté for about 5 minutes to crisp up. Add the remaining salt and the orange zest and juice and continue cooking, stirring continuously, for another 5–7 minutes.

Place some pork in the centre of each warmed tortilla and top with Pico de Gallo, Chipotle Slaw, spring onions, radishes and finish with some Apple Salsa.

BEEF BRISKET BARBACOA TACOS

Barbacoa is one of the most traditional and evocative meals as it is generally served at a celebration! Often a whole sheep or goat would be used, but beef brisket is used here.

100 g/3½ oz. red onions
300 g/10½ oz. large tomatoes
2 kg/4½ lb. trimmed beef brisket
4 tbsp paprika
2 tsp ground cumin
1 tbsp chopped chipotle chilli/chile
2 tsp avocado leaf powder
3 tsp salt
1 tsp freshly ground black pepper
2 tsp rice vinegar

Serve with

2 limes, cut into wedges
12 flour or corn tortillas, warmed
1 avocado, peeled, stoned/pitted
    and diced
Chargrilled Salsa (see page 120)

SERVES 4

Slice the red onions about 1 cm/½ inch thick. Slice the tomatoes into wedges.

Cut the beef into big chunks and place in a large lidded saucepan. Pour 2 litres/quarts water into the pan and add the onions, tomatoes, paprika, cumin, chipotle chilli, avocado leaf powder, salt, black pepper and rice vinegar. Mix together with a large spoon.

Place the pan over a high heat and bring to the boil, then cover with a lid and reduce the heat to low. Simmer gently for 3 hours, stirring occasionally and making sure the pan does not boil dry.

Shred the meat inside the saucepan using tongs or a fork. Just before serving, squeeze one of the limes over the shredded meat.

Put the meat on a tortilla, add some avocado, salsa and a squeeze of lime juice.

BEEF TONGUE TACOS

Don't be put off by the idea of beef tongue. It is like more common cuts of meat, but a bit fattier and milder than most. Boiling and softening it first is essential to avoid it becoming tough, but when prepared properly, it has a luxurious softness to it.

1 beef tongue, approx.
2 kg/4½ lb., cut into
4-5 pieces
3 dried chillies/chiles de árbol,
broken into 3-4 pieces
3 dried chillies/chiles guajillo,
broken into 3-4 pieces
3 garlic cloves, crushed
½ onion, sliced
1 tsp salt

Serve with
35 g/⅔ cup freshly chopped
coriander/cilantro
½ onion, finely chopped
Guacamole (see page 124)
2 limes, sliced into wedges
12-16 flour or corn tortillas,
warmed

SERVES 4

Place the beef tongue in a medium saucepan, add the chillies, garlic, onion, salt and 2 litres/quarts water. Cover with a lid. Bring to the boil over a high heat, then reduce the heat to low and simmer gently for 3 hours or until the tongue is tender and a knife goes into it easily. It has to be super tender for the best flavour. If necessary, top up the water during cooking to prevent the pan boiling dry.

Meanwhile, mix together the coriander and onion, make the guacamole, slice the limes into wedges and put to one side.

Take the cooked beef tongue out of the pan and discard the skin, which should peel off easily using tongs and a fork. If it does not, then it could probably do with a little extra cooking time. Chop the beef into small pieces and put in a serving bowl. Keep covered so that it stays nice and warm.

Place a warm tortilla on a plate, add some beef tongue pieces, sprinkle over some of the coriander and onion mix, squeeze lime juice on top and serve with a spoonful of the Guacamole.

GREEN MEATBALL TACOS

The mix of herbs and chillies/chiles brings a wonderful flavour to the meatballs. They also work really well with pasta.

500 g/1 lb. 2 oz. minced/
    ground beef
½ onion, finely chopped
3 garlic cloves, finely chopped
3 tsp freshly chopped mint leaves
1 tsp white pepper
1 tsp salt
40 g/⅔ cup dried breadcrumbs
2 tbsp vegetable oil
400 g/14 oz tomatillos
    (canned or fresh)
1 tbsp freshly chopped coriander/
    cilantro
1 green Thai chilli/chile, stem
    removed

Serve with
cooked rice
8-10 flour or corn tortillas, warmed
Avocado & Radish Salsa
    (see page 125)
Lime & Red Onion (see page 109)

SERVES 3–4

Place the beef, onion, garlic, a third of the mint, a third of the white pepper, a third of the salt and the breadcrumbs in a bowl and mix together well. Divide the beef mixture into 14 pieces, each weighing about 30 g/1 oz. Roll each piece into a ball and set aside.

Heat the vegetable oil in a large frying pan/skillet and brown the meatballs evenly for 2–3 minutes. Use a slotted spoon to transfer the meatballs to a plate lined with paper towels to soak up excess oil and wipe out the pan.

Put the tomatillos, coriander, Thai chilli and the remaining mint, white pepper and salt in a blender. Blend for about 1 minute.

Pour the mixture from the blender into the frying pan and sauté for 1–2 minutes, then add the cooked meatballs and 500 ml/2 cups water. Bring to the boil, then reduce the heat, cover and simmer for 7 minutes.

Place the warmed tortillas on a plate and top with the meatballs. Serve with a bowl of Avocado & Radish Salsa, Lime & Red Onion and the rice and dig in.

LAMB SHANK BIRRIA TACOS

Birria is a spicy stew traditionally made with lamb or goat, but beef or chicken can also be used, and is often made for special celebrations.

4 small lamb shanks, each
weighing approx. 350 g/12 oz.
15 g/½ oz. dried Guajillo chillies/
chiles, seeds and stems removed
2 garlic cloves, peeled
1 onion, chopped
300 g/10½ oz. tomatoes, chopped

Marinade
25 g/1 oz. fresh ginger, peeled
1 tbsp dried oregano
1 tsp ground cumin
1 tsp ground cinnamon
3 tbsp paprika
1 tsp freshly ground black pepper
1 tbsp salt
2 whole cloves
2 tbsp white vinegar

Serve with
12 flour or corn tortillas, warmed
your favourite salsas (see pages
108-125) and lime wedges

SERVES 4

Preheat the oven to 140°C/275°F/Gas 1. Put the lamb shanks into a large roasting pan and set aside.

Put the chillies, garlic, onion and tomatoes in a saucepan. Add 1.5 litres/6 cups water, bring to the boil and simmer for 5 minutes. Drain, discard the water and leave to cool.

Put all the marinade ingredients into a blender and blend. Then add the cooled chillies, garlic, onion and tomatoes and blend until you have a smooth purée.

Pour the blended mixture onto the lamb and spread over evenly, massaging it in with your hands. Cover the dish completely with foil, doubling-up to ensure there are no gaps. Cook in the middle of the oven for about 3-3½ hours until tender. Check occasionally and baste with some of the marinade from the base of the pan. The lamb should pull away easily with a little pressure from a fork – if it doesn't, cook for a little longer.

Pull the meat from the bones and shred, discarding the bones and fat and cover with foil to keep it warm.

Place the warmed tortillas in a stack on the table together with bowls of your favourite salsas and lime wedges and invite everyone to dig in.

ROASTED LAMB SHOULDER TACOS

The slow cooking of the lamb results in a meat bursting with flavour and when cooked to perfection, the juicy, tender meat falls off the bone.

1½ tbsp ground avocado
leaf powder

2 tsp salt

1 kg/2¼ lb. bone-in lamb
shoulder

Serve with

½ onion, finely chopped

20 g/1 cup freshly chopped
coriander/cilantro

Avocado Salsa
(see page 118)

Spicy Black Beans
(see Salmon & Spicy Black
Bean on page 58 but omit
the chile de árbol)

1 lime

6–8 flour or corn tortillas,
warmed

SERVES 3–4

Preheat the oven to 180°C/350°F/Gas 4.

In a large bowl, mix 60 ml/¼ cup water with the avocado leaf powder and salt. Place the lamb shoulder into the bowl and coat with the avocado leaf mixture.

Place a roasting rack over a medium roasting tray, place the meat on the middle of the rack and spoon over any remaining avocado leaf mixture. Pour 115 ml/½ cup water into the bottom of the roasting tray. Cover the lamb with foil. It is best to double-up to ensure that there are no gaps at the edges of the tray. Place in the preheated oven and cook for 2½ hours.

Mix the chopped onion and coriander together in a small bowl.

When the lamb is cooked and tender, remove from the oven. Leave to rest and cool a little for 10 minutes, then remove the meat from the bone (this should happen very easily), discarding any excess fat. Shred the meat.

Add a spoonful of the Spicy Black Beans to each warmed tortilla, then add the lamb. Spoon over the Avocado Salsa and sprinkle over lime juice and the onion-coriander mix.

CHAPTER 3

FISH & SEAFOOD

SPICY SHRIMP TACOS

This is a pretty simple dish and there are no overpowering flavours due to the way the prawns/shrimp are cooked. If you like a bit more heat, it is easy to adjust the spiciness by adding a little more crushed chilli/chile.

350 g/12 oz. medium raw
   shell-on prawns/shrimp
1 yellow (bell) pepper
1 red (bell) pepper
50 g/3½ tbsp butter
1 small onion, halved and then
   thinly sliced
4 garlic cloves, finely chopped
1 tsp crushed dried chillies/chiles
pinch of salt
2 tsp freshly chopped parsley

Serve with

50 g/½ cup finely chopped
   onion
35 g/⅔ cup freshly chopped
   coriander/cilantro
Avocado Salsa (see page 118)
12–16 flour or corn tortillas
2 limes, cut into wedges

SERVES 6–8

Peel the tails off the prawns, leaving the rest of them whole. Cut the yellow and red peppers in half and discard the stems, seeds and white ribs. Cut the flesh into 2 x 3-cm/¾ x 1¼-inch pieces.

To make the onion-coriander mix for serving, place the chopped onion and herbs in a serving bowl and mix together. Tip the Avocado Salsa into another serving bowl.

Start to warm the tortillas now as you want to be serving this dish with the prawns piping hot.

While heating the tortillas, put the butter in a saucepan and melt over a medium heat. Add the sliced onion, garlic, peppers, dried chillies and salt and cook for 4–5 minutes until soft. Add the prawns to the pan and cook for another 2 minutes, stirring, until the prawns are pink and cooked through.

Stir in the parsley and serve immediately with the warmed tortillas, the bowl of onion-coriander mix and the Avocado Salsa, and squeeze the lime juice over.

SHRIMP TACOS WITH BUTTER, GARLIC & PAPRIKA

Prawns/shrimp are perfectly suited to being a taco filling as they are so quick and easy to prepare and cook. The combination of flavours in this taco are best enjoyed with a cold beer dreaming of sunny holidays/vacations by the beach.

15 g/1 tbsp butter
2 garlic cloves, chopped
200 g/6½ oz. shelled raw or cooked
    prawns/shrimp
a pinch of paprika

Serve with
4 x 15-cm/6-in. flour or corn tortillas
150 g/2 cups shredded Romaine
    lettuce
Pico de Gallo (page 119)
Chipotle Garlic Mayonnaise (page 53)
1 lemon, cut into wedges

SERVES 2

Melt the butter in a frying pan/skillet over a low heat and fry the garlic, prawns and paprika for 2–4 minutes, stirring occasionally, until the prawns are cooked.

Place a dry frying pan over a high heat. Warm each tortilla for about 20–30 seconds on each side.

Layer up the ingredients over the tortillas: lettuce, Pico de Gallo, prawns and Chipotle Garlic Mayonnaise. Serve with lemon wedges to squeeze over.

FISH TACOS

Fish tacos are associated with Baja California, the Mexican peninsula with an incredible coastline that stretches for miles.

Chipotle garlic mayonnaise

2 garlic cloves, peeled
250 ml/1 cup mayonnaise
3–6 tbsp Chipotle chilli paste

Fish

125 g/1 cup plain/
    all-purpose flour
2 tsp paprika
2 tsp dried oregano
1 tsp dried marjoram
2 tsp ground cumin
½ tsp sea salt
½ tsp ground white pepper
4 tilapia fish fillets, each
    cut into 2 pieces
vegetable oil, for frying

Serve with

8 x 15-cm/6-in. flour or corn
    tortillas, warmed
shredded Romaine lettuce
Pico de Gallo (page 119)
1 lemon, cut into wedges

SERVES 4

Put all the ingredients for the chipotle mayonnaise in a food processor and blend until smooth. Set aside.

Put the flour, paprika, oregano, marjoram, cumin, salt, pepper and 250 ml/1 cup water in a large bowl and whisk together until very smooth and slightly thicker than double/heavy cream. Gently lower each portion of fish into the batter and make sure it is well coated. Set aside on a plate.

Pour some vegetable oil into a large, deep frying pan/skillet until it is 2 cm/¾ inch up the side of the pan. Set over a medium heat and leave until the oil is very hot but not smoking.

Using a slotted spoon, lower the portions of fish gently into the oil. Cook for 1–2 minutes on each side, depending on the thickness. Work in small batches – the fish should have plenty of room in the oil to fry evenly.

Using the tongs or a slotted spoon, remove the fish from the pan and allow to drain on paper towels. Repeat the process until all the portions have been fried.

Layer up the ingredients over the tortillas: lettuce, Pico de Gallo, the chipotle garlic mayonnaise and a portion of fish. Serve with the lemon wedges to squeeze over.

DEEP-FRIED FRESH TUNA TACOS

The flavour of the tuna and the bite of the radish salsa here are beautiful.

2 tomatoes, cut into wedges
1 fresh jalapeño, stem and seeds
removed
½ white onion, finely chopped
2 tbsp freshly chopped coriander/
cilantro
½ tsp salt
300 g/10½ oz. fresh tuna steak,
skin removed and flesh cut into
small chunks
½ a small cabbage, chopped
a pinch of freshly ground
black pepper
vegetable oil, for frying

Serve with

10 corn tortillas, warmed
Onion, Coriander & Radish Salsa
(see page 114)
diced avocado
200 g/7 oz. queso fresco or
feta cheese, cut into cubes
30 cocktail sticks/toothpicks

SERVES 4

Place 475 ml/2 cups water in a small saucepan with the tomatoes and jalapeño and bring to the boil. Turn down the heat and simmer for 4–5 minutes, then leave to cool. Once cooled, drain and transfer to a blender with half the onion, half the coriander and half the salt. Blend for 45–60 seconds, then set aside until ready to serve.

Put the tuna in a bowl with the remaining onion, half the cabbage and some salt and the black pepper. Mix well.

Place a tortilla on a flat surface, add one-tenth of the tuna mixture on one side and fold the other side on top. Secure with cocktail sticks. Repeat with the remaining tortillas and tuna mix.

Pour enough oil to reach a depth of about 2 cm/¾ inch in a frying pan/skillet. Heat the oil until very hot, but not smoking, then reduce the heat to medium. Deep-fry the tacos in batches for 3–5 minutes or until crispy, using metal tongs to turn them occasionally. Remove from the heat and lay them on paper towels to soak up any excess oil. When cool enough to handle, remove the cocktail sticks and top each one with some salsa.

Place 2–3 tacos on each plate, drizzle over the blended salsa, then sprinkle with the remaining cabbage, coriander, avocado and queso fresco.

CHIPOTLE TUNA TACOS

This chipotle tuna recipe makes a great filling for the crunchy taco shells, and can be put together from items you often already have in your store cupboard.

½ red (bell) pepper
½ yellow (bell) pepper
1 tomato
½ bunch of spring onions/scallions
⅓ medium romaine lettuce
240-g/9-oz. can of tuna, drained
75 g/½ cup sweetcorn/corn, drained
1 tbsp chipotle paste
3 tbsp freshly chopped coriander/cilantro
100 g/½ cup mayonnaise
700 ml/2⅔ cups vegetable oil

Serve with
8 corn tortillas
Jicama & Carrot Slaw (see page 90)

SERVES 3–4

Deseed and cut the red and yellow peppers into small chunks and dice the tomato. Thinly slice the spring onions and the romaine lettuce.

Place the vegetables in a bowl with the tuna, sweetcorn, chipotle paste, coriander and mayonnaise, and mix well.

Heat the oil in a large, deep frying pan/skillet over a medium-high heat. Carefully fold a tortilla in half, using tongs to keep it folded. Place it in the oil for a few seconds, starting with the bottom part (the fold) and then lay it on one side and then the other, frying until golden brown all over.

Remove the tortilla from the oil and drain on paper towels, then repeat with the remaining tortillas.

Place the taco shells on a serving plate. Fill with the tuna mix and top with the Jicama & Carrot Slaw.

SALMON & SPICY BLACK BEAN TACOS

This fish taco combines succulent oven-baked salmon with satisfying mashed black beans, pepped up with ginger and garlic.

Spicy black beans

165 g/1 cup dried black beans
3 tbsp vegetable oil
1-2 dried chillies/chiles de árbol,
   cut into small pieces
¼ onion, finely chopped
1 garlic clove, chopped
½ tsp salt
1 tbsp ground avocado leaf powder

Salmon

a splash of olive oil
500 g/1 lb. 2 oz. fresh salmon fillets,
   skin removed
½ tsp finely grated fresh ginger
a pinch of white pepper
2-3 garlic cloves, finely chopped

Serve with

12 flour or corn tortillas, warmed
Lime & Red Onion (see page 109)
fresh jalapeños, seeds and stems
   removed, thinly sliced

SERVES 4

Put the beans in a saucepan with 2 litres/quarts water and bring to the boil. Turn the heat down to low, partially cover and simmer gently for 2 hours. Check regularly to be sure there is still enough water and stir so that the beans don't stick to the bottom of the pan.

After 2 hours, heat the oil in a large saucepan over a medium heat. Add the dried chilli de árbol, onion, garlic, salt and avocado leaf powder and fry gently for 15-20 seconds. Mix together with the cooked beans. Transfer the beans and cooking water to a blender and blend for 1 minute. Tip into a saucepan and bring them back to simmer over a medium heat for about 2-3 minutes. Put to one side to cool.

Preheat the oven to 220°C/425°F/Gas 7. Line an ovenproof dish with foil and add a splash of olive oil. Place the salmon on the foil. Add the grated ginger and white pepper and scatter over the chopped garlic, gently pushing it into the fillets. Bake in the preheated oven for 20-25 minutes.

Once cooked, gently break the salmon into bite-sized pieces. Layer up the spicy beans over the warm tortillas, then add pieces of cooked salmon and top it up with the Lime & Red Onion and sliced jalapeños.

LOBSTER & CRAB FRITTER TACOS

Lobster is a special occasion food, but this recipe doesn't demand too much and the flavour comes through very well.

125 g/4½ oz. lobster meat
125 g/4½ oz. white crabmeat
3 tbsp freshly chopped parsley
2 garlic cloves, finely chopped
½ red onion, finely chopped
½ tsp salt
3½ tbsp freshly squeezed
    lime juice
50 g/heaping ⅓ cup plain/
    all-purpose flour
500 ml/2 cups vegetable oil

Serve with
sautéed courgette/zucchini slices
    (see Note below)
6 flour or corn tortillas, warmed
Chipotle Slaw (see page 87)
Pico de Gallo (see page 119)

SERVES 2–3

Chop the lobster and crabmeat into small pieces and put into a large bowl. Add the parsley, garlic, red onion and salt, then stir the mixture together. Add the lime juice and flour and mix again.

Form the mixture into small balls about 25 g/1 oz each, flatten each ball slightly, and arrange them on a sheet of baking parchment as you make them.

Pour the vegetable oil into a frying pan/skillet and heat, then when hot, fry the fritters in batches for 2 minutes, turning occasionally until golden. Drain the fritters on paper towels and repeat until you have fried them all.

Place the warmed tortillas on a plate, add a layer of Chipotle Slaw, lay three fritters on top, followed by the Pico de Gallo and finally the sautéed courgette slices.

Note: To prepare the sautéed courgettes, slice a courgette into thin strips using a peeler, and sauté in a pan with a splash of vegetable oil for 1 minute.

OCTOPUS & PARSLEY TACOS

These tacos combine tender cooked octopus with a parsley and garlic sauce which give it a wonderfully fresh flavour.

750 g–1 kg/1½–2¼ lb.
  cleaned octopus
1 bay leaf
10 black peppercorns
1 tsp salt, plus extra to taste
1 head/bulb of garlic, cut in
  half around its centre
2 lemons
2 tbsp extra virgin olive oil
freshly ground black pepper
2 tbsp freshly chopped
  parsley
1 tbsp finely chopped garlic

Serve with
12 flour or corn tortillas,
  warmed
Cucumber & Chilli Salsa
  (see page 21)
*12 wooden skewers, soaked
  in water for 5–10 minutes*

SERVES 4

Combine the octopus, bay leaf, peppercorns, salt, garlic head/bulb and 1 lemon, cut in half, in a saucepan along with enough water to cover. Turn the heat to medium, cover and bring to the boil. Once boiling, reduce the heat so that it simmers slowly and cook until the octopus is tender, about 45–60 minutes.

When the octopus is ready, it should cut easily with a sharp knife. Drain, discarding everything but the octopus, and set aside. You can prepare up to this stage 24 hours in advance and keep in the refrigerator.

Preheat the grill/broiler to medium-high. Cut the octopus into 2.5 x 2.5-cm/1 x 1-inch pieces, then thread them evenly onto the skewers.

Mix together the olive oil, pepper, chopped parsley and chopped garlic and brush this mixture evenly over the octopus. Place under the grill/broiler briefly, turning once, until the outsides brown but the insides are not dried out.

Cut the remaining lemon into wedges. Place the tortillas on a serving platter with a heap of the octopus skewers, the lemon wedges and the Cucumber and Chilli Salsa. One skewer is about right per taco (but don't forget to remove the actual skewer!).

CHAPTER 4

VEGETARIAN

TOFU TACOS

Tofu is not something that is eaten much in Mexico. It is very healthy though and its unique texture adds another dimension to many dishes. It also combines very well with a bit of heat. Pico de Gallo is the perfect accompaniment to these tacos, but you could serve them with sour cream too, if you like.

400 g/14 oz. tofu
½ red onion
1 red (bell) pepper
1 yellow (bell) pepper
2 garlic cloves
1 fresh jalapeño (or a couple
    of Thai green chillies/chiles
    for more heat)
20 g/1½ tbsp butter
½ tsp dried oregano
¼ tsp sea salt
¼ tsp ground white pepper
8 x 15-cm/6-in. flour or corn
    tortillas, warmed
Pico de Gallo (see page 119),
    to serve

SERVES 4

First, prepare the ingredients. Cut the tofu into strips about 5 cm/2 inches long. Cut the onion and peppers into strips and thinly slice the garlic and Jalapeño.

Melt the butter in a frying pan/skillet over a high heat, then fry the tofu for about 5 minutes.

Add the onion, peppers, garlic, oregano, salt and pepper and fry for 5 minutes. The tofu should be brown and a little crispy at the edges and the peppers should still have a little crunch. Stir in the chopped Jalapeño.

Spoon the ingredients over the tortillas and serve with Pico de Gallo.

TURMERIC & POTATO TACOS

The addition of turmeric turns the potatoes a pretty vibrant colour but don't let that put you off as they taste fantastic.

500 g/1 lb. 2 oz. potatoes, peeled and chopped into small pieces
1–2 fresh jalapeño chillies/chiles
3 tbsp vegetable oil
1 red onion, finely chopped
2 garlic cloves, chopped
½ tsp ground turmeric
¼ tsp dried oregano
2 tsp salt

Serve with
12 flour or corn tortillas, warmed
Red Cabbage Mix (see page 86)
Pico de Gallo (see page 119)
100 g/3½ oz. Cheddar cheese, cubed

SERVES 4–6

Place the chopped potatoes in a saucepan of boiling water and boil for 8-10 minutes until tender. When the potatoes are cooked, drain them and set aside.

Cut the jalapeño chillies in half, remove the seeds and thinly slice.

Place 2 tablespoons of the oil in a frying pan/skillet over a medium heat. Add the onion, garlic and jalapeño slices and sauté for 1 minute. Add the cooked potatoes and sauté for 5–6 minutes.

Add the turmeric, oregano and salt and continue cooking for another 2–3 minutes, gently stirring with a spoon. Finally, add the rest of the oil and cook the mixture for another minute, before removing from the heat and placing on the side, ready to serve.

Spread the potato mixture in the middle of the warmed tortillas. Top them with the Red Cabbage Mix, Pico de Gallo and the cubed Cheddar cheese.

POBLANO CHILLI STRIP TACOS

Poblanos are not always easy to find, so feel free to use (bell) peppers, but using ripe poblanos will add a whole new dimension to this dish.

4 poblano chillies/chiles
2 tbsp vegetable oil
1 tbsp butter
1 onion, sliced
150 g/¾ cup sweetcorn/corn
a pinch of salt
a pinch of white pepper
125 ml/½ cup sour cream
125 g/1½ cups grated/
    shredded Manchego
    cheese

Serve with

Red Chunky Salsa
    (see page 108), with an
    added spalsh of olive oil
12 flour or corn tortillas,
    warmed
7–8 radishes, thinly sliced
100–150 g/¾–1 cup feta
    cheese, crumbled
freshly chopped coriander/
    cilantro

SERVES 4–6

Roast the chillies over the flame of the stove, using tongs, until the skin has evenly burned. Place them in a clean plastic bag, wrap the bag in a towel and let them rest until they have cooled.

Then, using a paper towel, peel the skin from the chillies (you can also put the chillies in a bowl of warm water to help peel off the skin). Slice open the chillies, discard the stems and seeds and slice into long, thin strips.

Heat the oil and butter in a saucepan over a medium heat and sauté the onion until transparent, then add the sliced chilli and sweetcorn. Season with the salt and white pepper and cook for 3–5 minutes.

Reduce the heat and add the sour cream and Manchego cheese. Stir to melt the cheese, then turn off the heat immediately and serve.

Add a splash of olive oil to the Red Chunky Salsa before serving. Add a spoonful of creamy poblana strips to the centre of each warmed tortilla, sprinkle on the sliced radishes, then the Red Chunky Salsa and crumbled feta, and finally garnish with chopped coriander.

SAUTÉED ASPARAGUS TACOS

This simple mix highlights the delicate flavours of the vegetables and balances it with the creamy, tartness of the feta cheese for a dish full of colour and flavour.

60 ml/¼ cup vegetable oil
500 g/1 lb. 2 oz. asparagus,
    woody ends removed
¼ red onion, sliced
1 courgette/zucchini, cut into 5-mm/
    ¼-inch thick half-moon slices
1 red (bell) pepper, deseeded and sliced
1 yellow (bell) pepper, deseeded
    and sliced
a pinch of salt
a pinch of freshly ground
    black pepper
2 garlic cloves, finely chopped
1 dried chilli/chile de arbol, finely
    chopped
2 tbsp freshly chopped parsley

Serve with
12 flour or corn tortillas, warmed
Fresh Salsa (see page 108)
feta cheese, crumbled

SERVES 4–5

Add the oil to a frying pan/skillet, bring it to a high heat and sauté the asparagus for 2–3 minutes. Add the onion, courgette, peppers, salt and pepper to the pan and continue to sauté for another 3 minutes. Finally, stir in the garlic, chile de árbol and parsley and stir continuously for another 1–2 minutes.

Pile the filling in the middle of the warmed tortillas, add the salsa and sprinkle some feta cheese on top.

SPICY WILD MUSHROOM TACOS

You can be as adventurous as you like with this delicious, spicy mix of sautéed wild mushrooms, butter, fresh garlic, fresh ginger, pepper and a touch of heat.

125 g/4½ oz. fresh, mixed wild or shiitake mushrooms
125 g/4½ oz. button mushrooms
½ small red (bell) pepper
½ small yellow (bell) pepper
¼ onion
1 large garlic clove, very finely chopped
15 g/½ oz. fresh ginger, very finely chopped
2 tsp freshly chopped parsley (leaves only)
1½ tsp crushed dried chillies/chiles
1 tsp salt
30 g/¼ stick butter

Serve with
8-10 flour or corn tortillas, warmed
mixed spring leaves, such as watercress, spinach and rocket/arugula
Pico de Gallo (see page 119)
salad dressing (optional)

SERVES 4

Wash the mushrooms and slice them 1 cm/½ inch thick. Cut the red and yellow (bell) pepper halves and discard the stems, seeds and white ribs. Cut into pieces about 3 cm/1¼ inches square. Slice the onion into strips about 1 cm/½ in thick.

Place the prepared vegetables in a bowl, add the garlic, ginger, parsley, dried chillies and salt and stir to mix well.

Put a saucepan over a high heat and melt the butter for about 1 minute. Then add the mushroom mixture, stir together and sauté for 6–8 minutes.

Place a warm tortilla on a plate, add a layer of mixed leaves, followed by a small spoonful of Pico de Gallo and top with a generous spoonful of the wild mushrooms. Serve with additional mixed leaves and a simple oil and vinegar dressing, if you wish.

SPICY LENTIL TACOS

Lentils absorb aromatic spices so well and have here been combined with cumin, paprika and oregano for a punchy flavour.

200 g/1 cup uncooked green
lentils, washed and drained
2 tbsp vegetable oil
1 large onion, diced
4 garlic cloves, finely chopped
1 fresh jalapeño chilli/chile, diced
200 ml/scant 1 cup vegetable stock
75 g/½ cup sweetcorn/corn
2 tsp paprika
¼ tsp ground cumin
¼ tsp freshly ground black pepper
1 tsp dried oregano
1 tsp salt

Serve with
10 corn tortillas
12 cherry tomatoes, chopped
½ head cos lettuce, thinly sliced
½ jicama/yam bean, peeled
and grated
Guacamole (see page 124)
beetroot/beet dip (optional)

SERVES 4

Preheat the oven to 180°C/350°F/Gas 4.

Put 600 ml/2½ cups water in a saucepan, add the lentils and bring to the boil. Reduce the heat, cover and simmer for 20 minutes until the lentils soften. Drain.

Heat the oil in a saucepan and sauté the onion, garlic and jalapeño for 2–3 minutes over a medium heat, stirring frequently, until the onion starts to turn brown and translucent.

Add the cooked lentils, vegetable stock, sweetcorn, paprika, cumin, black pepper, oregano and salt and bring to the boil. Reduce the heat to low, cover and simmer for 5–7 minutes, stirring frequently and adding more water, 1–2 tablespoons at a time, as needed, to stop the vegetables sticking to the pan.

Drape each corn tortilla over two bars of a horizontal oven shelf so that the tortilla's two opposing sides hang down evenly, facing each other. Bake the tortillas for 5–7 minutes until crisp. Remove the tortillas from the oven shelf and admire your new taco shells.

Spoon the lentil mixture into the taco shells and top with the tomatoes, lettuce, jicama bean, Guacamole and beetroot dip, if using.

CAULIFLOWER & CHICKPEA TACOS

The combination of cauliflower and chickpeas/garbanzo beans makes a healthy taco. These are easy to make, full of protein, taste great and the presentation of them looks pretty special too!

1 red onion, chopped
2 garlic cloves, chopped
1 tsp paprika
½ tsp ground cumin
½ tsp sea salt
½ tsp dried oregano
1 tbsp olive oil
250 g/1½ cups canned chickpeas/
    garbanzo beans, drained
1 small cauliflower, cut into florets
1 carrot, peeled and finely diced

Serve with

50 g/½ cup finely chopped
    onion
35 g/⅔ cup freshly chopped
    coriander/cilantro
12–16 flour or corn tortillas, warmed
Avocado Salsa (see page 118)
6 radishes, thinly sliced
baking tray, greased

SERVES 6

Preheat the oven to 200°C/400°F/Gas 6.

Place the red onion and garlic in a medium bowl with the paprika, ground cumin, salt, oregano and oil along with 2 tablespoons of water and mix well.

Add the chickpeas, cauliflower and carrot to the mixing bowl and stir the mixture to make sure the vegetables are covered with the seasoning.

Spread out the mixture on the greased baking tray and roast in the preheated oven for 35–40 minutes until the cauliflower is tender.

Mix the chopped onion and coriander together in a bowl. Place a generous spoonful of the cauliflower mixture on each warmed tortilla and serve with the onion-coriander mix, the Avocado Salsa and sliced radishes.

ROASTED PUMPKIN TACOS

Pumpkins are a versatile and underused ingredient that can work equally well in savoury and sweet dishes, but butternut squash could also be used.

1 kg/2¼ lb. fresh pumpkin, peeled, deseeded and cut into small cubes
4 tbsp olive oil
1 tsp salt
1 tsp freshly ground black pepper
1 tsp ground cumin
1 tsp ground avocado leaf powder
1 tsp chilli/chili powder
½ red (bell) pepper
½ yellow (bell) pepper
¼ red onion
2 garlic cloves, peeled
75 g/½ cup sweetcorn/corn

Serve with
10–12 flour or corn tortillas, warmed
beetroot/beet dip (optional)
Toasted Pumpkin Seeds (see page 91)

SERVES 4–5

Preheat the oven to 220°C/425°F/Gas 7 and place a roasting tray inside to heat up.

Place the cubed pumpkin in a large bowl and add 2 tablespoons of the olive oil, and half of the following ingredients: salt, pepper, cumin, ground avocado leaf powder and chilli powder. Mix well, making sure that all the pumpkin pieces are thoroughly coated.

Scatter the mixture on the preheated roasting tray. Bake in the oven for about 20–25 minutes or until the pumpkin is soft and charred at the edges.

Cut the red and yellow peppers in half and discard the stems, seeds and white ribs. Cut the peppers into small pieces.

Chop the onion and garlic and mix with the peppers. Add the sweetcorn and the remaining olive oil, salt, pepper, cumin, ground avocado leaf powder and chilli powder and mix well. Add to the roasting tray of pumpkin, stir well and bake for another 15–20 minutes. Stir it a few times during baking to be sure it is evenly roasted.

Put a good spoonful of the cooked pumpkin mixture in the middle of each warmed tortilla and serve with the beetroot dip, if using, and the Toasted Pumpkin Seeds.

DEEP-FRIED AVOCADO TACOS

The crispy-on-the-outside/creamy-soft-in-the-centre avocado wedges combine beautifully with the spicy Chipotle Slaw, fresh Pico de Gallo, sharp squeeze of lime juice and the tart crunch of fresh radishes. A mouth-watering dish if ever there was one.

2 avocados, halved, stoned/pitted and sliced lengthways
135 g self-raising flour/1 cup all-purpose flour mixed with 2 tsp baking powder
1 tsp ground avocado leaf powder
2½ tsp ground cumin
4 tsp dried oregano
3 tsp paprika
½ tsp white pepper
½ tsp salt
1 bottle (330 ml/1½ cups) Sol beer (or similar crisp lager)
vegetable oil, for frying

Serve with
6 flour or corn tortillas, warmed
Chipotle Slaw (see page 87)
Pico de Gallo (see page 119)
2 limes, each cut into 4 wedges
thinly sliced radishes

MAKES 6

Put the flour into a large bowl. Add the avocado powder, cumin, oregano, paprika, pepper and salt and mix together well. Make a well in the centre, add the beer and mix gently until you have a smooth batter.

Fill a small saucepan with vegetable oil to a depth of about 7–8 cm/2¾–3¼ inches and place over a medium-high heat, or heat a deep fat fryer to 180°C/350°F.

Coat the avocado slices in the batter, then carefully lower them into the hot oil and deep-fry for 30 seconds on each side until puffy and crisp, taking care not to burn them. Fry a few slices at a time.

Remove the avocado slices from the oil with a slotted spoon and place on a plate lined with paper towels to absorb any excess oil.

Layer up the warmed tortillas with the avocado fritters, Chipotle Slaw, Pico de Gallo and a squeeze of lime juice, and garnish with thinly sliced radishes. Serve with additional slaw and the remaining lime wedges.

CHAPTER 5

SIDES
& SALSAS

RED CABBAGE MIX

The cabbage retains a very satisfying crunch if this is served soon after having been made, but it can be left to stew and soften in the fridge for several days if preferred. A very simple and tasty accompaniment to vegetarian and seafood dishes.

100 g/3½ oz. red cabbage
1 tbsp olive oil
2 tbsp balsamic vinegar
a pinch of salt
a pinch of freshly ground
    black pepper

SERVES 6–8

Cut the red cabbage in half and then finely slice each half, discarding any tough stems.

Place in a bowl and add the olive oil, balsamic vinegar, salt and black pepper and mix well.

CHIPOTLE SLAW

Here, smoke-dried jalapeño (known as a chipotle) provides a delightful gentle heat to go with creamy mayonnaise and crunchy vegetables.

2 tsp chipotle paste
1 garlic clove, peeled
150 g/¾ cup mayonnaise
125 g/4½ oz. white cabbage
60 g/2½ oz. red cabbage
1 carrot

SERVES 6–8

Place the chipotle paste, garlic and mayonnaise in a blender and blend together for just under 1 minute.

Slice both cabbages as finely as you can, discarding any tough stems. Place in a bowl.

Peel the carrot, chop off the ends and discard, then grate into the bowl containing the cabbage.

Mix together the carrot and cabbage, and then combine with the mayonnaise from the blender and mix well.

Red Cabbage Mix

Chipotle Slaw

Jicama &
Carrot Slaw

Toasted
Pumpkin Seeds

JICAMA & CARROT SLAW

Jicama, also known as yam bean, is rather like a Mexican turnip. It is usually eaten raw, often just sprinkled with a little lime juice, and has become a very popular salad ingredient.

½ jicama/yam bean
1 carrot
freshly squeezed juice of 1 lime
a pinch of salt
a pinch of freshly ground
    black pepper

SERVES 6–8

Peel and grate the jicama/yam bean. Peel and grate the carrot, then combine the two in a large bowl.

Squeeze the juice of the lime over the mixture, add the salt and pepper and mix well.

TOASTED PUMPKIN SEEDS

These are known as pepitas, and you'll see people munching on them on every street in Mexico's bustling cities. Eat them to keep you going through the day, make them your spicy, salty go-to snack to have with a cold drink, or sprinkle them over a simple green salad.

140 g/1 cup pumpkin seeds
½ tsp ground paprika
¼ tsp salt
1 tbsp vegetable oil

SERVES 6–8

Place a saucepan over a medium heat, add the pumpkin seeds and toast for 5–7 minutes in the dry pan until they give off a toasted aroma, stirring continuously.

Turn off the heat and add the paprika, salt and vegetable oil and mix well.

Place a paper towel on a plate and tip the pumpkin seeds onto the plate so that any excess oil can be absorbed. After a few minutes, tip the seeds into a serving bowl.

BEER-BATTERED AVOCADO DIPPERS

This combination of crispy batter and soft avocado is amazing.

6-8 ripe avocados, peeled,
    stoned/pitted and sliced
    into 3-4 pieces lengthways
vegetable oil, for deep-frying

For the batter
165 g self-raising flour/1⅓ cups
    all-purpose flour mixed with
    2 tsp baking powder
1 tsp salt
1 tsp ground cumin
1 tsp dried oregano
1½ tsp paprika
½ tsp freshly ground black pepper
1 tsp ground avocado leaf powder
1 tsp baking powder
1 bottle (330 ml/1½ cups) lager
    of choice

**For the chipotle
mayonnaise**
150 g/¾ cup mayonnaise
2 tsp chipotle paste
1 garlic clove, peeled

SERVES 6–8

First, make the batter. Mix together all the dry ingredients until they are well combined. Gently stir in the beer until you have a smooth batter, then put to one side.

Put all the ingredients for the mayonnaise in a blender and blend for 1 minute until smooth. Set aside.

Pour enough oil into a medium saucepan to reach halfway up the side and heat until hot but not smoking.

Working with one avocado at a time, dip the slices in the batter until well covered, then carefully lower into the oil – it's best to use a slotted spoon to do this to avoid spitting oil.

Fry each batch for about 1 minute so that the batter is golden coloured, but no darker, and crispy. Remove with a slotted spoon and place on a plate lined with paper towels to soak up any excess oil. Repeat with the remaining avocado slices.

Transfer the chipotle mayonnaise to a serving bowl and place on a large serving plate. Arrange the avocado slices on the plate, serve and watch your friends' amazement when they try this dish!

ROASTED CHERRY TOMATOES

This is an understated dish with few ingredients, but the fresh basil leaves and tomatoes work wonderfully together. Serve as an appetizer in the middle of the table and watch your guests devour them, or have it as an accompaniment to many of the dishes in this book.

1 punnet of cherry tomatoes
(about 330 g/11 oz.)
olive oil, for drizzling
¼ tsp sea salt
¼ tsp freshly ground
black pepper
15 fresh basil leaves,
chopped

SERVES 4

Preheat the oven to 200°C/400°F/Gas 6.

Place the tomatoes in a mixing bowl, add some olive oil and mix well.

Put the tomatoes on a baking tray, sprinkle the salt and pepper over them and roast in the preheated oven for 15–20 minutes, until the tomatoes are soft.

Transfer the tomatoes to a serving platter and sprinkle with chopped basil leaves.

SAUTÉED ONIONS WITH CHILLIES

This simple side dish can be used to add fire to any meal. 'Toreados' comes from the word 'torear', meaning to bull fight. Here it describes the reaction that happens when you sauté chillies, thereby increasing their spicy kick.

10–15 fresh jalapeños or chillies/
    chiles de árbol/Thai green chillies
1 onion, thinly sliced
1 tbsp olive oil
1 lime or lemon, cut into wedges
2 pinches of sea salt

SERVES 6–8

Cut any particularly large chillies in half lengthways but otherwise leave them whole.

Heat the oil in a saucepan and fry the chillies and onion for 2–3 minutes.

Remove from the heat and squeeze the lime or lemon into the pan.

Season with the salt and mix together well. Taste and add more salt if required.

Note: Jalapeños are perfect for adding to Mexican dishes or scattering over pizzas. However, buy them fresh and you will better appreciate their fiery flavour. They are small and plump with a thick flesh and you will usually find them green, although if left to ripen on the plant, they turn red. They are wonderful thrown into potent salsas.

REFRIED BLACK BEANS WITH AVOCADO LEAVES

Black turtle beans are a staple of Mexican cuisine and are here beautifully enhanced by the aniseed flavour of avocado leaf powder. Feel free to use star anise or fennel seeds if you can't find any though.

175 g/1 cup dried black
   (turtle) beans
1 tbsp vegetable oil
¼ onion, finely chopped
1 garlic clove, finely chopped
1 tsp avocado leaf powder
a pinch of sea salt

SERVES 4–6

Put the dried beans and 2 litres/8 cups water in a deep saucepan. Bring to the boil, then turn the heat down to low, partially cover and simmer gently for 2 hours. Check every 30 minutes to be sure there is still enough water and stir so that the beans don't stick to the bottom.

After 2 hours, heat the oil in a large saucepan over a medium heat and fry the onion, garlic and avocado leaf powder for 1 minute.

Add the beans and their cooking water and cook until they start to boil, then turn the heat down to low, add the salt and cook for 10 minutes, crushing the beans regularly with a potato masher. Taste and add more salt if required.

REFRIED BLACK BEANS WITH CHORIZO

This versatile refried beans recipe is taken to a new level with the addition of chorizo and feta cheese – deliciously smoky, with the feta cutting through the strong flavours perfectly.

1 quantity cooked
   black (turtle) beans
   (see page 99)
1 tsp vegetable oil
100 g/3½ oz. chorizo,
   thinly sliced
200 g/2 cups crumbled
   feta cheese
sea salt

SERVES 4–6

Cook the beans according to the instructions on page 99.

Put the oil in a non-stick frying pan over a medium heat – you only need a very small amount because the chorizo will release some of its own oils on cooking.

Add the chorizo and fry for about 1–2 minutes, then remove half the chorizo from the pan and set aside.

Add the beans and their cooking water to the pan and cook until they start to boil, then turn the heat down to low and cook for 10 minutes, crushing the beans and chorizo regularly with a potato masher. This will blend the flavours beautifully. Taste and add salt if required.

Sprinkle the reserved chorizo and some crumbled feta over the top to serve.

REFRIED PINTO BEANS
WITH PAPRIKA

You will be hard pressed to find a restaurant in Mexico that does not serve its own version of this classic.

175 g/1 cup dried pinto beans
½ tsp sea salt
1 tbsp vegetable oil
¼ onion, finely chopped
1 garlic clove, crushed
2 tsp paprika

SERVES 4

Put the dried beans and 1.5 litres/6 cups water in a saucepan. Bring to the boil, then turn the heat down to low, partially cover and simmer gently for about 2–2½ hours. Add a little more water if necessary. You should be able to crush the beans easily.

Heat the oil in a large saucepan over a medium heat and fry the onion and garlic for a few seconds.

Add the beans, their cooking water and the paprika and cook for 10 minutes over medium-low heat, mashing continuously with a potato masher. Add a little extra boiling water if dry, and taste and add more salt if required.

NORTHERN-STYLE REFRIED PINTO BEANS

This is for meat lovers – using sausages, frankfurters and pancetta. It is my own rich and hearty take on the popular 'frijoles charros', or cowboy beans.

1 quantity cooked pinto beans
    (see opposite)
100 g/3½ oz. good pork sausages
3 frankfurters
100 g/3½ oz. pork belly or pancetta
¼ onion
2 tomatoes
1 small bunch of fresh coriander/
    cilantro
1 tbsp vegetable oil
1 tsp sea salt

SERVES 4

Follow the first paragraph from the recipe opposite and then continue here.

Cut the sausages and frankfurters into small, equal chunks. Finely chop the pork belly or pancetta, onion, tomatoes and coriander.

Put the oil in a saucepan over a medium-high heat and fry the pork belly or pancetta for 5–7 minutes, stirring regularly, until browned. Add the sausages and fry for 5 minutes or until well done. It is important that these ingredients are cooked through.

Add the onion and frankfurters and fry for 1 minute. Add the salt and the beans, together with their cooking water, bring to the boil and cook for 2 minutes. Turn the heat down to low, add the tomatoes and coriander and simmer for 10 minutes.

When ready, the liquid should have a slightly creamy consistency. Add a little extra boiling water if dry, and taste and add more salt if required.

Northern-style
Refried Pinto Beans

Coriander-Lime rice

Sautéed Rice with Spring Veg

CORIANDER-LIME RICE

Rice forms the foundation of most Mexican meals so it's particularly important to give it proper care and attention and not serve it in the same plain way every time. Follow this recipe and you will get beautiful, fluffy rice with fresh lime and coriander and earthiness from the white pepper.

2 tbsp vegetable oil
200 g/1 cup basmati rice
¼ onion, finely chopped
a pinch of sea salt
a pinch of ground white pepper
1 bunch of fresh coriander/cilantro, finely chopped
1 tbsp lime juice

SERVES 2

Heat the oil in a deep saucepan, then fry the rice, onion, salt and pepper over a low heat for about 2–3 minutes, stirring continuously.

Add 500 ml/2 cups water, cover with a lid and cook for about 8–10 minutes or according to the pack instructions. After it has been boiling for about 5 minutes, carefully taste the cooking water – this will give you a good idea of what your rice will taste like, so add more seasoning now if necessary.

Stir in the coriander and lime juice just before serving.

SAUTÉED RICE WITH SPRING VEG

This rice dish is supposed to be based on whatever you have in the garden but ultimately, it is about throwing in as many and as varied vegetables you like to make a full, flavourful and tasty rice dish.

¼ red onion
2 garlic cloves
2 carrots
2 tbsp vegetable oil
400 g/2 cups basmati rice
100 g/3½ oz. wild or oyster
    mushrooms
1 tsp sea salt
¼ tsp ground white pepper
1 vegetable stock cube
100 g/3½ oz. baby corn
100 g/1 cup mangetout/snow peas
4 green chillies/chiles

SERVES 4

Thinly slice the onion and garlic. Cut the carrots into matchsticks.

Heat the oil in a large saucepan over a medium heat, then fry the rice, onion, garlic, mushrooms, salt and white pepper for 3–5 minutes.

Dissolve the stock cube in 1 litre/4 cups boiling water and add to the pan with the carrots, baby corn, mangetout and chillies. Boil for about 2 minutes, then turn down the heat to low, cover with a lid and simmer gently for 10 minutes or according to the pack instructions.

FRESH SALSA

The perfect all-rounder – a light and fresh salsa with a little kick of heat.

1 kg/2¼ lb. fresh tomatoes
250 g/9 oz. canned peeled plum
   tomatoes
50 g/¼ cup finely chopped onion
10 g/¼ cup fresh Thai chillies/chiles,
   finely chopped
20 g/½ cup freshly chopped
   coriander/cilantro
3 tsp salt

SERVES 6–8

Cook the fresh tomatoes in a pan of boiling water for 12–15 minutes. Drain and leave the tomatoes to cool.Once cooled, remove the skins and put the tomatoes in a bowl with the plum tomatoes. Squash the tomatoes with your hands (wear plastic gloves for this), then remove any big pieces and finely chop with a knife before adding them back into the bowl.

Add the onion, chillies, coriander and salt and mix well to combine.

RED CHUNKY SALSA

A delightful mix to serve with almost anything.

½ red (bell) pepper
¼ red onion
a splash of olive oil
1 tabs freshly chopped coriander/
   cilantro

SERVES 6–8

Cut the pepper and onion into chunks, add a splash of olive oil and the coriander and mix well.

LIME & RED ONION

A delicious salsa served with fish and pork.

2 red onions
2 tbsp vegetable oil
1 fresh jalapeño chilli/chile
2 tbsp freshly squeezed lime juice
a pinch of dried oregano
1 tsp salt

SERVES 6–8

Cut the onions in half and then cut them into 5-mm/¼-inch thick slices.

Put a small saucepan over a medium heat, add the oil and fry the onions and whole jalapeño for about 1 minute, stirring continuously to cook it evenly. Be careful not to let the mixture stick and overcook.

Remove the onions and jalapeño from the saucepan and put in a small bowl. Allow to cool, then add the lime juice, oregano and salt and mix well.

Fresh Salsa

Lime &
Red Onion

Red
Chunky
Salsa

Tropical Pineapple Salsa

Apple Salsa

TROPICAL PINEAPPLE SALSA

This is a wonderful salsa to serve with pork or simple vegetable dishes. The combination of sweet pineapple with very hot habaneros is spectacular but not for the faint-hearted!

2 tbsp vegetable oil
100 g/3½ oz. yellow (bell) peppers, cored, deseeded and roughly chopped
¼ onion, roughly chopped
300 g/10½ oz. fresh pineapple chunks
100 g/3½ oz. Scotch bonnet chillies/chiles (habaneros)
2 tsp salt, or more to taste
300 ml/1¼ cups rice vinegar
3½ tbsp agave syrup

SERVES 6–8

Put the oil in a frying pan/skillet set over a medium heat, add the yellow peppers, onion and pineapple and sauté for about 15 minutes.

Remove from the heat, add 300 ml/1¼ cups water and set aside to cool.

Once cool, transfer the ingredients to a blender, add the chillies, salt, rice vinegar and agave syrup and blend for about 2 minutes until smooth. Taste and add more salt if required.

Cover the salsa and keep in the refrigerator as it is best served chilled.

APPLE SALSA

A fresh and tangy salsa for lovers of apple sauce.

300 g/10½ oz. Golden Delicious apples
3 tbsp olive oil
7 g/⅛ oz. dried chilli/chile de árbol, stem removed
¼ red onion, finely chopped
1 tbsp freshly squeezed lime juice
250 ml/1 cup unsweetened apple juice
2 tsp salt
1½ tsp freshly chopped coriander/cilantro

SERVES 6–8

Peel and core the apples. Cut into quarters, then roughly chop the quarters into 5-mm/¼-inch squares.

Put a non-stick saucepan over a high heat, add 2 tablespoons of the olive oil and sauté the apple pieces for about 10 minutes until charred and caramelized, then set aside to cool.

Set another non-stick saucepan over a medium heat. Add the remaining oil and sauté the chilli de árbol for about 30 seconds, then remove with a slotted spoon and set aside. Add the red onion to this oil, sauté for 30 seconds, then set aside to cool.

Put the sautéed apples, lime juice, cooked chilli de árbol, apple juice and salt into a blender and blend for 1 minute.

Pour the mixture from the blender into a bowl, add the sautéed red onion and fresh coriander and mix well before serving.

ONION, CORIANDER & RADISH SALSA

Quick, easy and very colourful, this salsa brightens up your table and adds a crisp and refreshing bite to your tacos.

5 tbsp finely chopped onion
2 tbsp freshly chopped coriander/
   cilantro
1 bunch of radishes, thinly sliced

SERVES 6–8

Put all the ingredients into a bowl and mix together well to combine.

Note: Coriander/cilantro has such a distinctive, pungent taste that it invokes very strong opinions – both positive and negative! Those who like it rave about the fresh, clean fragrance it adds to dishes, especially spicy ones. Add it at the end of a recipe so that its flavour isn't lost in cooking. This is a herb to enjoy raw and zingy.

TOASTED CHILE DE ÁRBOL SALSA

Take care when toasting the chillies/chiles as they give off a strong aroma. Don't let this put you off though – the smell will have your mouth watering.

2 dried chillies/chiles de árbol,
    stems removed
2 fresh tomatoes
1 garlic clove, peeled
¼ tsp salt

SERVES 6–8

Place a saucepan over a medium heat, add the dried chillies de árbol and toast for about 1 minute (they should be charred on all sides and give off quite a strong smell), then set aside.

Place the tomatoes and garlic in a dry saucepan and toast them for 4-5 minutes, turning them several times to cook evenly, but keep the lid on when you are not turning them.

Put all the ingredients in a blender with the salt and blend for 1 minute, then tip into a serving bowl.

If you think the salsa is a little runny, you can thicken it by pouring it into a frying pan/skillet and simmering gently.

Onion, Coriander & Radish Salsa

Toasted Chile de Árbol Salsa

Avocado Salsa

Pico de Gallo

AVOCADO SALSA

A medium-spicy salsa with a wonderful creamy texture, great with lamb or beef tongue tacos.

100 g/3½ oz. whole green tomatillos (fresh if possible, but canned will do)
1-2 fresh green chillies/chiles (such as serrano or Thai green), stems removed
2 garlic cloves, peeled
1 avocado
1 tsp freshly chopped coriander/cilantro (the thin stalks can be used, just discard the thicker ends)
1 tbsp finely chopped onion
a pinch of salt

SERVES 6–8

Preheat the oven to 200°C/400°F/Gas 6.

Remove the husks from the fresh tomatillos. Place the whole chillies, garlic and tomatillos on a baking tray and roast in the preheated oven for about 6–8 minutes until all are slightly charred on the outside. (If using canned tomatillos, there is no need to roast them, simply add them at the next stage.)

Cut the avocado in half and remove the stone. Using a spoon, scoop out the avocado flesh and put it in a blender. Add the roasted chillies, tomatillos (or canned if using) and garlic, coriander, onion and salt and blend for 2 minutes. Up to 60 ml/¼ cup water can be added if it seems too thick. Add more salt to taste if required.

PICO DE GALLO

When these fresh, simple ingredients are combined together, they produce a wonderful salsa bursting with flavour. Like other Mexican salsas, there are many variations, such as adding lime juice and fresh chillies/chiles.

4 tomatoes
¼ onion
¼ bunch of fresh coriander/
    cilantro
¼ tsp sea salt

SERVES 6–8

Finely chop the tomatoes, onion and coriander. Place in a bowl and mix well, then add the salt and mix again.

CHARGRILLED SALSA

A great example of a salsa that would work equally well as a dip or a sauce. Charring the ingredients gives a light, smoky flavour.

250 g/9 oz. tomatoes
100 g/3½ oz. tomatillos
(fresh if possible, but canned can also be used)
250 g/9 oz. large onion
2-3 garlic cloves, peeled
2 tbsp olive oil
10 g/⅓ oz. dried chilli/chile de árbol, stem removed
a pinch of salt, or to taste

SERVES 6–8

If using canned tomatillos, leave them out of these first stages and simply add them in at the blender stage.

Preheat the grill/broiler to a high heat.

Cut the tomatoes and fresh tomatillos in half. Cut the onion into about 4 big pieces. Place the tomatoes, fresh tomatillos, onion pieces and garlic on a baking tray and grill/broil for about 5-10 minutes, or until they are gently charred. Set aside to cool.

Put a non-stick frying pan/skillet over a medium heat, add the olive oil and sauté the chilli de árbol for about 30 seconds. Then add 60 ml/¼ cup water, remove from the heat and set aside to cool.

Put all the ingredients, apart from the salt, into a blender, including the canned tomatillos if using. Blend for about 30 seconds until combined but slightly chunky. Transfer to a serving bowl and add salt to taste.

SMOKED CHIPOTLE SALSA

You can adjust the amount of chillies/chiles you use here to taste – this recipe is for medium-hot.

100 g/3½ oz. tomatoes,
    cut into wedges
½ onion, cut into pieces
2½ tbsp vegetable oil
1 tbsp crushed dried chillies/chiles
70 g/¼ cup chipotle paste
1 tbsp agave syrup
1 tbsp salt
60 ml/¼ cup rice vinegar
¼ tsp freshly ground black pepper
¼ tsp ground cumin
¼ tsp dried oregano
½ tsp hickory powder

SERVES 6–8

Put the tomatoes, onion and 250 ml/1 cup water into a saucepan, bring to the boil and simmer for 5 minutes. Drain and discard the cooking water and set the tomatoes and onion to one side.

Place the vegetable oil in a saucepan over a medium heat, add the crushed dried chillies and fry for 1–2 minutes, being very careful not to let them burn. Add the tomatoes and onion right at the end, then remove from the heat and set aside to cool.

Transfer the cooled mixture to a blender, add all the remaining ingredients and blend until smooth.

Put a saucepan over a high heat, add the mixture from the blender and bring to the boil. Boil for about 1–2 minutes, adding up to 100 ml/scant ½ cup water if the mixture is too thick.

This salsa is best served cold so allow time for it to cool or put in the fridge before serving.

*Smoked
Chipotle
Salsa*

*Chargrilled
Salsa*

*Avocado &
Radish Salsa*

Guacamole

AVOCADO & RADISH SALSA

This dish takes some of the most used, but also contrasting, ingredients in Mexican cooking, and simply puts them together. Creamy avocado, tart radish and onion, sharp lime and a little chilli/chile heat, for a colourful, refreshing salsa.

1 large avocado
7-8 radishes
½ small onion
15 g/¼ cup fresh coriander/cilantro
1 fresh jalapeño chilli/chile
    (stem removed)
freshly squeezed juice of 1 lime
¼–½ tsp sea salt, to taste

SERVES 6–8

Cut the avocado in half, remove the stone, scoop out the flesh and dice it.

Thinly slice the radishes. Finely chop the onion, coriander and jalapeño.

Combine the avocado, radishes, onion, coriander and jalapeño in a bowl and stir. Sprinkle the lime juice and salt on top and mix again.

Note: Avocados are native to central Mexico. Now one of the most traded tropical fruits in the world, Mexico remains the biggest producer. Anyone who is a fan of this rich, creamy fruit (mostly but not exclusively used in savoury dishes) has tried guacamole or a variation at least once and fallen in love with its fresh, zingy flavour.

GUACAMOLE

Guacamole is one of the most well-known dishes, its origins dating back to the sixteenth century. The recipe varies throughout Mexico, but this version helps the flavour and texture of the avocados shine through as much as possible.

2–3 avocados
1 bunch of fresh coriander/cilantro
a pinch of sea salt
a pinch of ground white pepper
1 tomato

SERVES 6–8

Cut the avocados in half, remove the stones and scoop the flesh out into a bowl.

Finely chop the coriander and add to the bowl with the salt and pepper. Roughly mash with a fork.

Finely chop the tomato and stir into the guacamole.

INDEX

ABOUT THE AUTHORS

FELIPE FUENTES CRUZ was born in Puebla, Mexico, and has worked as a chef in the US, Spain, London and Mexico. While working in a London restaurant, he met **BEN FORDHAM**. They quickly realized they shared the same dream of bringing great Mexican food to London and, in 2008, Benito's Hat was created. In 2017 Felipe and Ben launched a new street food venture, bringing tacos (these simple, handheld bundles of Mexican deliciousness) to the masses. Felipe went on to open Doña Nata Mexican Kitchen, his own, solo venture in Los Cabos, Mexico.

ABOUT THE PHOTOGRAPHER

PETER CASSIDY is one of Europe's most talented photographers. He specializes in food and travel and his work frequently appears in magazines. For Ryland Peters & Small, he has photographed many books including *The Red Hot Chilli Cookbook, The ScandiKitchen* and *The Tomato Basket*

ADDITIONAL PICTURE CREDITS

All photography is by Peter Cassidy, except for the following:

Helen Cathcart: *page 86.*

Steve Painter: *pages 79, 107 and 109.*

Christopher Scholey: *page 72.*

Ian Wallace: *page 119.*

Kate Whitaker: *pages 33, 68, 106 and 112.*

Clare Winfield: *pages 25, 50, 114 and 125.*